THE
COMPLETE BOOK
—OF—
BONSAI

THE
COMPLETE BOOK
——— OF ———
BONSAI

An Inspirational Guide

Peter Chan

Photography by Don Wood

BRACKEN BOOKS

THE COMPLETE BOOK OF BONSAI
is published 1989 by Bracken Books
an imprint of Bestseller Publications Ltd.,
Princess House, 50 Eastcastle Street,
London W1N 7AP, England.

ISBN 1 85170 287 3

The Complete Book of Bonsai
was conceived, edited, designed and
produced for Bracken Books Ltd. by
Morgan Samuel Editions
4 Somerset Road, London W13 9PB.

Editorial: Thomas Paul, Emma Worth
Design: Tony Paine, Sarah Macdonald
Iona Macglashan
Publisher: Nigel Perryman

Typeset in 10/12pt and 11/14pt Ehrhardt by Highbridge Printing, London
Separations by Scantrans, Singapore
Printed and bound by Slovart, Czechoslovakia

CONTENTS

INTRODUCTION

There can be few people today who will not have heard of bonsai: they are increasingly seen in garden centres and department stores, and are quite often used as props for television programmes – you can even buy artificial versions of these beautiful trees if you cannot afford the real thing.

Bonsai is certainly becoming more popular all the time: no longer is the art confined to China and Japan. There is now a bonsai following in almost every country in the world. The countries that you would least expect to have an interest in bonsai commonly have a thriving club devoted to this absorbing pastime. There are no racial, social or geographical barriers – people all over the world now find pleasure and relaxation in the hobby.

And yet it was not very long ago that bonsai was a novelty to most Westerners. I can still recall the early 1960s, when visitors to the famous Chelsea Flower Show in London used to flock around the bonsai stands because the trees were considered a great novelty. That bonsai has come of age is demonstrated by the fact that the first ever World Bonsai Convention was held in Omiya in Japan in April 1989. I and many other bonsai enthusiasts from all over the world were privileged to attend this historic event.

There are many theories as to why bonsai has become so popular in recent years. To my mind, there are three main reasons: first, we live in a shrinking world; second, there has been an explosion of interest in oriental culture; and, last, a bonsai appeals to the ordinary person because it is a beautiful thing. Other reasons for the increasing popularity of bonsai include the peace and tranquillity that bonsai can impart, and the suitability of bonsai for town and suburban gardens, which are becoming smaller and smaller. People keep bonsai for a variety of reasons, but perhaps the most compelling of them is the intrinsic and timeless beauty of these miniature trees.

As with any interest or pastime, bonsai can become a way of life. For many people bonsai starts off as an innocent hobby – but over a period of time it becomes an obsession. One's way of life becomes geared to bonsai – holidays, pets, and so on. Some may go so far as to give up their careers to devote the rest of their life to this hobby.

Making bonsai is a creative experience of the highest order. It is sheer enjoyment. I experience a "high" every time I make or see a fine bonsai tree. I am sure that this is not unique to bonsai – anyone who has had an obsession for any other pursuit will know precisely what I mean. But it is my hope that my love for bonsai can be communicated to the reader through the pictures of my trees and the commentary contained in this book. It is meant to be an inspirational guide – one that makes the art of bonsai come alive. With experience, dedication and a good eye for composition, you too will be able to produce trees of which you can be proud. Remember, though, that bonsai is an art, and, as with any of the arts, the enjoyment of creation, hard work and – sometimes – frustration are all a part of the total experience.

Contemporary bonsai, like Ikebana, has some very noble aims. One of the main ones is to stimulate international friendship and to bring peace through the common bond of love for beauty. The peace and tranquillity that bonsai can impart is widely recognised by both bonsai enthusiast and non-enthusiast alike. If they were to be multiplied several times over on every continent then the world would be a less tense and a considerably happier place.

Peter Chan
Heron's Bonsai Nursery, April
1989

THE PRINCIPLES OF BONSAI

INTRODUCTION
History and Culture.

BONSAI AS ART
A Miniaturization of Nature.

GROWING BONSAI
Basic Requirements and Every-day Care – Pruning
Roots – Watering – Feeding – Placement.

BONSAI AESTHETICS
Composing the Picture – Styles and Shape – Pots.

The display area at Herons Nursery in Newchapel,
Surrey. Bonsai should always be displayed against
a neutral background, such as this bamboo
screen, and ample space should be left between
the trees.

THE TRADITION

HISTORY AND CULTURE

Bonsai has a long and ancient history. As with most of the oriental arts, bonsai originated in China and then spread eastwards to Japan via Korea. The knowledge was spread by Buddhist monks. From ancient manuscripts and paintings, we know that artistic pot plants were being cultivated by the Chinese around 600AD, but some scholars think that bonsai, or at least potted plants, were being grown in China as far back as 500 or even 1,000BC. Bonsai first appeared in Japan during the 12th century

There are a number of reasons why bonsai originated in China. As a race, the Chinese have always loved flowers and plants, and the country is naturally endowed with a rich diversity of flora. In fact, most of the cultivated plants that are grown in the West today have their origins in China's "Middle Kingdom". The Chinese also had a passion for gardens, and in some of their gardens they recreated scenery that they had seen in the mountains. Many of these gardens were on a miniature scale and included numbers of miniature shrubs and trees, planted to reinforce the scale and balance of their landscapes. But the Chinese were also interested in miniaturization as a science in its own right. They believed that miniature objects had concentrated within them certain mystical and magical powers.

Finally, the development of Chinese ceramics must have played a major part in the development of bonsai as we know it today. Without the beautiful Chinese pots, bonsai trees would not have been admired as much as they have been. After all, a *bonsai* literally means "a tree in a pot". The two together must form a single entity. Even to this day, the most highly sought after containers for the finest bonsai in Japan are very often antique Chinese pots.

Over the centuries, though, bonsai has developed along quite different lines in China and Japan. Chinese bonsai is still very much in the ancient mould – the shapes and styles are traditional and may appear even crude

A group of 21 Japanese white beeches, *Fagus crenata*, imported from Japan in 1987. Just 35.5 inches (90cm) wide, the composition has perfect balance.

to Western eyes. The Japanese style of bonsai is much more naturalistic and pleasing. Japanese trees are also much more refined and better groomed. It would be wrong to say that one style of bonsai is better than the other. It is simply that the two are so very different. Both, of course, have their own very definite and particular charm.

Much of the bonsai that has been seen in the West since the early 1950s is Japanese in origin. The social and political changes in China between the '50s and late '70s were not conducive to the promotion of bonsai as an art form. Of course, this is not to say that the Chinese peasantry and ordinary Chinese people did not continue to grow bonsai for their own enjoyment. Even during the years of the Cultural Revolution the art of bonsai was being practised, although the authorities would not have viewed it as a productive or economic activity. Today, the situation is quite different. China has a thriving and vigorous bonsai export industry that is making significant inroads into Western markets. The monopoly that Japan has enjoyed until now is coming to be shared with a number of other countries, though the quality of Japanese trees continues to be of the very highest order.

We owe a great debt to the Chinese and Japanese for developing this fascinating art, and, what is more, for keeping the art alive for almost 2,500 years. Without their enthusiasm and artistic guidance, we would not be enjoying bonsai as we know it today. It is not simply the horticultural tradition for which we are indebted, but the philosophy and mental attitudes that accompany this art. The aesthetic sensibilities of bonsai, which have their roots in the Zen tradition, contribute very significantly to the total experience of bonsai – which in essence is about beauty, peace and tranquillity.

A particularly good example of red maple, *Acer palamatum,* of the "Deshojoh" variety, with the carmine red leaves of early spring, grown in the twin-trunk style.

BONSAI AS ART

A MINIATURIZATION OF NATURE

Bonsai is becoming increasingly recognized as an art form. Bonsai is not simply horticulture, although this is the basis on which the art is built. In horticulture, the prime objective is to grow plants that have attractive foliage and flowers: in bonsai these same physical attributes are important, but it is the aesthetic quality which is paramount.

Bonsai is an art form in the same way that painting and sculpture are art forms. Just as a painter captures a beautiful landscape on a piece of canvas, so, in the same way, a bonsai artist recreates on a miniature scale what he or she sees in nature. It may be a beautiful single specimen tree, or a massive forest consisting of many trees. The painter's medium might be oils or pastels, but for the bonsai artist the raw material is ordinary, living plant material. However, the analogy between painting and bonsai ends here, because, once completed, a painting does not need much more doing to it. The bonsai artist's work is never complete, because it is alive and growing. It needs constant care and attention in order to keep it in perfect condition. A bonsai, therefore, is never static: it can change – either for the better or the worse.

Bonsai masterpieces are valuable because they are collectors' items. In Japan, famous trees change hands for vast sums of money. Even trees that are not so famous, but have been shown at major bonsai exhibitions, increase in value, simply because they are well on the road to fame. There is a tradition in Japan that famous bonsai masterpieces are owned by wealthy individuals and large corporate institutions. The title to the trees may remain with the owners, but they are kept at the bonsai nursery in which they have been grown so that the Bonsai Master can care for them properly. This is done not so much for convenience, but because there is a great respect for the well-being of the trees – which in many cases are very, very old.

Just as famous paintings are produced by great painters, so bonsai masterpieces are created by great Bonsai Masters who have particular

This Chinese rock landscape harks back to the
origins of bonsai, in Chinese landscape
representation.

styles that can be recognized. This is because a bonsai artist attempts to capture the spirit and mood of a particular tree, by a subtle bend of a branch here, and a twist there, so the artist's personality and perceptions play their part. It is said that great artists – and bonsai artists come into this category – are born and not made. But this is not to say that the ordinary bonsai enthusiast cannot strive for perfection. It is the creative process that is most important. To own and to enjoy a finished bonsai represents a different, and higher, level of experience.

Even very ordinary bonsai are relatively expensive when compared with their counterparts in the horticultural trade. But, when it comes to high quality bonsai, the difference is even more marked. There are two reasons for this; first, all bonsai take a long time to produce; second, good-quality bonsai are works of art. Just as a good painting cannot be valued simply on the basis of the cost of its raw materials, so, by the same token, a good bonsai cannot be valued on the strength of its intrinsic worth as a pot plant. The price of any work of art is a highly contentious issue, that of bonsai is no exception. But, at the end of the day, it is not so much the monetary value of a work that is important: rather it is the pleasure and experience that one derives from it that counts.

A mountain landscape, or *san-sui,* made from
Chinese grey slate. About 15 inches (40cm) high, it
takes its inspiration from the mountains of Western
China.

GROWING BONSAI

BASIC REQUIREMENTS AND EVERY DAY CARE

Bonsai has always been steeped in mystery. Consequently, many myths and misconceptions have grown up over the years. One general misconception is that a bonsai is some special, genetically engineered species of tree. Of course, this is not true: almost any tree or shrub can be dwarfed and made into a bonsai. In fact, bonsai are ordinary trees and shrubs that have been miniaturized by skilful horticultural techniques. But these techniques are not too onerous, being similar to those for ornamental plants and shrubs grown in containers. If this is borne in mind then much of the worry of keeping bonsai can be overcome and work with them becomes a pleasure rather than a chore.

Although it is possible to use certain dwarf varieties of conifers for bonsai, it is not absolutely essential to do so. The range of trees and shrubs suitable for bonsai is quite vast, and the choice depends to a large extent on personal preference. Some species are more suitable than others, and they are usually the ones that have small foliage so that the leaves are in keeping with the scale of the tree when dwarfed. Bonsai should be regarded very much as ordinary trees and shrubs that are grown in pots: the only difference being that they are artistically trained and shaped. The pots are, of course, somewhat special. Once this principle is grasped, then the mystique of bonsai vanishes, and the cultivation of these lovely trees becomes less of a mystery.

Another myth that has grown up is that bonsai are starved in order to restrict their growth. Again, this quite wrong: bonsai are fed regularly and to be successful must be in the very best of health. The trees shown in this book – all from my collection – are all in tip-top condition. This can only be achieved through meticulous care and attention to the feeding requirements of individual trees. Feeding is essential, because bonsai, though small, are still growing plants. In fact, bonsai should be fed more regularly than their counterparts in nature, because their pots are much smaller. Consequently, the nutrients in their soil become exhausted sooner.

This superb mountain maple, *Acer* spp., won a high
certificate of merit at the Nippon Bonsai
Association's Osaka Exhibition in 1988.

PRUNING ROOTS

But perhaps the most common belief that prevails today is that one has to prune the roots regularly in order to keep a bonsai dwarfed. While there is some element of truth in this, the idea is a gross distortion of what is generally practised. In itself, pruning of roots does not dwarf a tree. In fact, it is a combination of pruning of branches and restriction of roots in a container that miniaturizes a tree.

The roots of a bonsai are pruned when the tree requires repotting. This happens only when the tree becomes pot-bound, or when the bonsai artist wants to put the tree in a slightly larger pot. The main purpose of pruning the roots is to introduce fresh soil into the pot. By doing this the roots will have more room to grow, and so will be better able to breathe and to take up water and nutrients more efficiently.

There are no hard and fast rules about the frequency of root-pruning and repotting, because some varieties of trees grow more quickly than others. The more vigorous varieties, such as trident maple, hornbeam and cotoneaster, require pruning once a year. Other varieties, such as pines and junipers, require repotting less frequently – once every two to five years, say. As a general rule, the older a tree the less frequently it needs to be repotted. Some of the specimen trees shown in this book are well over 100-years old, and are only repotted once every five or six years. Even then, only a small amount of the root is removed.

If the tree is growing healthily, and the roots are not pushing the tree out of its pot, there is no need to un-pot the tree to prune its roots. Root-pruning does set the tree back to some extent, and it should always be done with great care. In any event, a tree should be protected for two to three weeks after repotting, in order that it can re-establish itself. Ideally, repotted trees should be sheltered from strong draughts and frosts – a cool greenhouse or conservatory is ideal.

WATERING

Watering is perhaps the most important of all the aspects of bonsai-care. All too frequently, bonsai trees die as a result of not being watered regularly. Because a bonsai is a living plant, it needs to be watered almost daily during the growing season. During summer, this means watering the tree at least once a day, or sometimes two or three times a day if the weather is very hot and dry. Preferably, you should water your trees in the late evening after the sun has gone down, or in the early morning before the sun begins to shine on the leaves. But trees should not be stood in

This powerful looking Chinese Juniper, *Juniperus chinensis* "Sargentii", is about 100 years old, and stands some 27.5 inches (70cm) high.

water permanently, since the roots need air to breathe.

One or two varieties of tree, however, actually benefit from such treatment, because they are naturally fond of water: trees such as willow, alder, wisteria and swamp cypress thrive if they are stood in a bowl of water during the summer, though these are perhaps the only species that should be treated in this way. In all other cases, trees should be allowed to drain freely after each watering.

It is said that watering is an art that is acquired over many years. The point is that watering should never be done haphazardly. It is not sufficient to rely on a passing shower of rain, for example, to water your bonsai. Very often the heavy canopy of leaves does not allow rain-water to even penetrate the surface of the pot. The only way to water a tree properly is to use a watering can or a garden hose. The tree should be drenched with water two or three times: each time for about thirty seconds, so that water soaks through the pot completely. Allow an interval of about two minutes between each soaking, and remember that the foliage benefits from being sprayed with water as well.

FEEDING

Bonsai should be fed regularly – and that means either every fortnight or once a month. But you should only feed your trees during the growing season: in other words, ordinary, temperate-climate hardy trees should be fed from late spring right through to late summer. However, you can start to feed evergreens slightly earlier than this, and continue feeding for a little longer – perhaps no more than a month each way. Indoor bonsai may need feeding regularly throughout the year, because the trees are continually in growth. Be sparing with the fertilizer, as overfeeding can sometimes make a tree sick, and only use it as the manufacturers recommend.

PLACEMENT

The placement of your bonsai is important, too. Again, common sense should prevail. Your tree should be kept in a spot that only receives the sun for part of the day. Although it is possible to grow bonsai in full sun, a tree will require much more care and attention during the summer. The ideal position for your bonsai is a spot that gets the sun for three or four hours each day. A position near the house is probably as good a place as any: this will give protection both from fierce sunshine, strong winds and cold draughts.

A massive specimen Japanese Grey Bark elm,
Zelkova serrata, grown in a style that recalls the
pollarded oaks of the English countryside.

It is important to keep your bonsai in a position in which it can enjoy the benefits of rainfall, for tap water should not be used all the time. During the winter, protect your trees as far as possible from draughts and frosts: a cool greenhouse or conservatory is ideal, but otherwise a sheltered spot near the house is probably adequate – a garden patio, for example, where your family and friends can enjoy the trees. Large collections of bonsai can be displayed on wooden staging raised off the ground, which can be adapted to provide an overhead shelter during the winter months.

A 27-year-old Japanese Grey Bark elm, *Zelkova serrata*, grown in the traditional broom style.

BONSAI AESTHETICS

COMPOSING THE PICTURE

For most people the attraction of bonsai lies in the beauty of the form and shape of these tiny trees. It is not so much the foliage or the flowers that catches the eye, as, say, in the case of fuchsias or orchids. This is why bonsai is regarded as an art-form rather than as horticulture. The design of the trees follows well-established aesthetic principles, governing line and form, mass and visual balance, perspective and depth and so on. All these principles are used with great subtlety and skill to achieve an end result that is pleasing to the eye.

The fundamental point to remember when creating a bonsai is that you are composing a picture. The bonsai artist tries to reproduce on a miniature scale what is seen in nature. He or she is, in fact, trying to create an illusion of full grown trees using ordinary plant material. How successfully this is done depends primarily on the artist's creative talent. Every twist and bend to the trunk and branches is done deliberately to create the desired shape and form. The bonsai artist draws inspiration from nature, but the end result depends on how he or she interprets the conceived image in tangible form.

STYLES AND SHAPE

A bonsai must look like a proper tree if it is to be convincing. Consequently, it must have a trunk – because all trees have trunks. If the trunk is absent, or not clearly visible, then it will look like an ordinary bush or garden plant. Like a person's body, a bonsai trunk is a feature that attracts immediate attention. The way the trunk is shaped establishes what is known as the "trunk line". This may be slanting, upright, windswept, curved like an "S", and so on. In fact, the trunk is considered to be so important that all the recognized styles in bonsai are named after its configuration.

Although it may not be immediately apparent, most bonsai have a front and a back. The front, or viewing side of a tree is more open and shows

A group of 15 Korean Hornbeams, *Carpinus turczaninovi*. These trees are particularly suited to group planting.

off the trunk to best advantage. The back of the tree has more branches at the rear – these serve as a foil or backdrop to set off the trunk, and create depth and perspective. Very few bonsai are designed to be viewed from all sides, and most bonsai are created specifically with a definite front and a back in mind.

The overall shape of a bonsai is what determines its form and visual mass. Most bonsai are triangular in shape. The triangle is widely used as the basic form because it gives the appearance of stability and repose. An inverted triangle, on the other hand, with its apex pointing downwards, does not convey this feeling of stability. As long as you design your tree in what is essentially a triangular shape your composition should be pleasing.

The disposition of the branches is perhaps the next most important factor in bonsai aesthetics. By convention, branches emerge from the outside of the elbows of bends along the trunk. Seldom will you find a branch emerging from inside a bend. Branches should be distributed evenly along the length of the trunk, but remember that the front of the tree should be kept fairly open. The twigs that emerge from a branch form what is known as a foliage pad. This should be flat like the palm of your hand. Shoots should not hang down downwards or grow upwards to spoil the flat line of this pad.

The roots of a bonsai are also very important in the overall design. They should be visible on the surface near the trunk, so that they give the impression of gripping the soil firmly. A trunk that emerges straight from the soil would not look as convincing: in fact, it would simply look like a telegraph pole stuck into the ground.

POTS

The shape and size of the bonsai pot in relation to the size and height of the tree is another crucial factor in bonsai design. As a general rule, the depth of the pot should be in direct proportion to the thickness of the trunk. The length of a pot is usually about two-thirds the height of the tree, so trees that have thick trunks look right in chunky looking deep pots, while thinner and more slender trees look better in shallower pots. The shapes of the pots themselves are really a matter of taste. Although they are determined to a large extent by convention and fashion, your personal opinion – what looks right to your eye – is what matters in the end. Remember the Chinese proverb: "rules are for the observance of fools, but provide guidance for the wise". So do not follow the rules and conventions of bonsai too slavishly. There is scope for improvization in

This Japanese maple, *Acer palmatum,* of the
"kashima" variety, is about 65 years old.

bonsai, and it is in fact by occasionally breaking these rules and conventions that true creativity results, to give a new and refreshing insight into the art.

A small *cotoneaster,* grown from a seed around 14
years ago, set off by small netsukes aaround 0.5
inches (1.5cm) high.

BONSAI STYLES
AND SPECIES

BONSAI STYLES

A Means to an End – Ezo Spruce – Larch – Chinese Elm – Globosa Pine – Kashima Maple – Trident Maple – Larch – Hinoki Cypress – Cotoneaster – Chinese Juniper – Nandina – Sageretia – Nandina – Zelkova Nire – Bamboo – Nandina – Trident Maple – Trident Maple – Mountain Maple – Japanese Hornbeam – Juniper – Scots Pine – Firethorn – Maple – Trident Maple – Chamaecyparis – Shikoku White Pine – Trident Maple – Kiyohime Maple – Zelkova Serrata – Nishiki Black Pine – Mame Juniper – Sawara Cypress – Zelkova Makino – Three Zelkovas – Scots Pine – Japanese Hornbeam – Juniper Rigida – Needle Juniper – San Jose Juniper – Japanese Black Pine – Trident Maple – Japanese White Pine.

Grown in the formal-upright style, this larch was collected as a young seedling 20 years ago and is now 19.6 inches (50cm) high. Though wired occasionally, no leaders have ever been cut, and the beautiful conical shape is entirely natural.

BONSAI STYLES

A MEANS TO AN END

To the layman, one bonsai is very much like another. But to the enthusiast each and every tree is different. Some bonsai have straight trunks and some are slanting; some have single trunks; others have two or more trunks; and so on. There is a multiplicity of shapes and configurations, all of which add to the richness and variety of the art.

Throughout the Chinese and Japanese bonsai tradition, artists have always been aware of the need to clarify the various shapes and styles, and a system of nomenclature has evolved to categorize them. One convention is to group trees according to the number of their trunks, giving these major groups: single-trunk styles, multiple-trunk styles, and the multiple-tree, or forest styles.

Within each of these groupings there are sub-divisions, based on the shapes of the trees. So the single-tree group, for example, includes the formal-upright style, informal-upright, driftwood, windswept, root-over-rock, weeping, cascade style and so on. The multiple-trunk group has the same sub-divisions as the single-trunk group; while the multiple-tree, or forest group described groups of trees that have been planted on rock or made into landscapes. In all, about 30 to 40 distinct styles of bonsai are recognized today.

The important point to remember, though, is that styles in bonsai are only a means to an end. Their purpose is to describe trees more easily and to serve as a common language for bonsai enthusiasts. They should not be seen as the determining factor in the design of the trees. In bonsai, shapes are first and foremost the images of trees as seen by the bonsai artist. These may be inspired by nature, or by merely subliminal images of tree shapes that have

Juniperus chinensis "San Jose".

left a lasting impression on the artist. Once the bonsai artist has created the shapes, the viewer can proceed to classify them into the various styles. Sometimes, of course, a tree does not fit any of the conventional styles – but this does not mean that the tree has no artistic merit, or is not a true bonsai.

THE RULES OF BONSAI

The system of classification based on the various codified styles has led to the development of the so-called "rules" for styling. This has given rise to some very rigid practices in the way the branches and roots of a tree are arranged and also in the choice and shapes of the pots. The true bonsai artist has long been aware of this danger: an artist should not bound by the rules but should have the wisdom and intellect to determine what is appropriate and what is not.

So remember that these "rules" of bonsai can be broken, and doing so often results in the creation of the great masterpieces. Avoid, too, the trap into which many bonsai enthusiasts fall: looking for faults in trees, based on their own – sometimes limited – knowledge of the rules. This is a negative approach to a positive art.

The examples of the various styles in this section of the book were all photographed at our Nursery in Newchapel, Surrey. They are by no means all masterpieces, because many superior specimens are to be found in China and Japan. But they are good examples, and it is my hope that they will serve as an inspiration to bonsai artists.

Cycas revoluta.

EZO SPRUCE

A GROUP PLANTING

This group of five Ezo spruce *(Picea Glehnii)* is 33.8 inches (86cm) high and the pot is 27.5 inches (70cm) wide. The trees are fairly old – probably around 65 years – and the group was imported from Japan in the early 1960s, when this species was still permitted into the UK by licence. It was originally part of a much larger forest planting consisting of 39 trees. Over the years it has been taken apart and this is all that remains of a massive group.

This variety of spruce is a favourite of Japanese bonsai enthusiasts, and is quite easy to propagate from cuttings: over the years I have grown hundreds of young plants from the five parent trees. On the other hand, an Ezo spruce is difficult to train, but when developed well the result can be stunning.

When I acquired the group in 1980, it was in very poor condition, but with careful nurturing it has now been restored to some of its former glory and looks natural and well-composed. It is one of the most admired forest plantings in my collection and when it is exhibited at 'Chelsea' it seldom fails to draw attention. This is partly because forest and group plantings are very popular with the general public, to whom they epitomize all that is appealing and natural about bonsai.

Five *Picea glehnii*

LARCH

A WINDSWEPT STYLE

This larch was collected from a peat bog in Scotland 16 years ago. The growing conditions there were so harsh that most of the tree was dead, and only one side was still alive.

It was planted in a large tub filled with peat and sharpsand, which encourages fibrous roots to develop, and within a year the tree began to put out new growth. In the third year it was planted in a bonsai container, the process of designing the tree was begun. Because the tree only had one live branch, it was a natural subject for the windswept style, so I created the shari and also refined some of the jins by carving the tree with a fine model-maker's router.

The image that results is of a tree that grows near the coast and is constantly battered by the wind: trees such as this can often be found on the Cumbrian coast, in England, and also in North West Scotland. They are all one-sided and lean with the wind in order to survive. This stark beauty of this bonsai – around 33.5 inches (85cm) wide and 25.5 inches (65cm) high – is much admired at shows.

A *Larix* from a Scottish peat bog.

CHINESE ELM

AN INFORMAL-SLANTING STYLE

This Chinese elm is not particularly old – perhaps no more than 25 or 30 years – and is around 25.5 inches (65cm) high, with a trunk diameter of 9.8 inches (25cm). It was grown by cutting down a much larger tree, and the tapering effect has been achieved by repeatedly cutting each year's new leader back to 2 inches (5cm) each time.

The branches have been grown over the last four or five years and the overall design is already very pleasing, with the spread of roots and trunk undoubtedly being the focus of attention. The root-spread is very impressive and conveys the impression of immense stability. Notice how guidewires have been used to keep the foliage pads horizontal.

Ulmus parviflora.

GLOBOSA PINE

BRANCH STRUCTURE

This pine was developed from ordinary nursery material seven years ago. The precise variety is *Pinus Sylvestris Globosa Viridis* – not an easy tree to train into a bonsai, since it is reluctant to put out good branches.

Left to its own devices, this tree grows into a rounded bush made up of thin shoots that emerge from the main trunk. The branch structure on this bonsai was developed from the thickest of the shoots found on the tree and the rest of the weaker shoots were simply removed. By constant pinching of the growing tips, new shoots have been forced to develop further back into the old wood.

The result is a tree with a very pleasing shape. The foliage pads on the branches are getting denser and the crown, too, is becoming more mature and rounded. Now the tree measures 28.7 inches (73cm) and rather resembles a Japanese black pine. It sits in a stoneware container that I made a few years ago.

Pinus sylvestris globosa viridis.

KASHIMA MAPLE

A SPECIMEN TREE

It is said that in bonsai, time and patience are the pre-requisites for creating great masterpieces. Both ingredients have certainly been lavished on this stunning tree – a specimen Japanese Maple imported from Japan in 1988, and now 33.5 inches (85cm) wide and 27.5 inches (70cm) high.

The kashima variety of maple has very small leaves and short internodes. When kept well pinched, it develops a very dense twig structure and progressively smaller leaves. This specimen tree is 85cm wide and 70cm high.

Acer palmatum "kashima"

TRIDENT MAPLE

ROOT-OVER-ROCK STYLE

The trident maple (*Acer Buergerianum*) is probably the most popular species to use when one wants to train a bonsai in the root-over-rock style – as can be seen from this illustration and the ones on the next few pages. Tridents grown in this style come in many different shapes and sizes, from around 8 inches (20cm) to 3.25 feet (1m) high. This 45-year-old tree is of average size, being 23.5 inches high (60cm) and weighing nearly 5 stones (30kg) – it takes two people to lift it on to the display bench.

Trees grown over rock are always fascinating, because as their roots develop so many interesting shapes and patterns. The shape and texture of the rock are important, too, because they add to the richness of the composition: in this case, the rock's vertical shape helps to make it look like a tall tree.

Acer buergerianum.

TRIDENT MAPLE

ROOT-OVER-ROCK STYLE

This large trident maple – about 23.5 inches (60cm) high – gives one the impression of a rider on horseback. Root-over-rock bonsai only work well when both tree and rock form one harmonious entity – and, of course, the pot has to complement the effect.

This composition does work, because that synthesis has been achieved. The rock has character, the tree is beautiful, with a powerful root structure, and the pot suits both elements to form a pleasing unity.

Acer buergerianum.

TRIDENT MAPLE

ROOT-OVER-ROCK STYLE

This trident maple is about 30 years old and 17.5 inches (45cm) high; it was imported from Japan in 1988. Even though trident maples are good subjects for growing in the root-over-rock style, since their roots quicken thickly, this style of bonsai does take many years to develop. It can take anything from six to ten years for the roots to clasp the rock strongly, and when this has happened the canopy develops over the next four to five years. So expect to work with the tree for between 10 and 15 years before you succeed in producing a good-looking root-over-rock bonsai.

Acer buergerianum.

LARCH

ROOT-OVER-ROCK STYLE

Trees grown on rock are always eye-catching. They appeal because they have a natural, rugged appearance, with the rock and the tree usually combining well together to create a harmonious composition.

This larch, now nearly 20 inches (58cm) high, has been trained over a rock since 1970, when it was collected from the wild – it is probably between 40 and 50 years old, and still bears cones regularly. It has been trained in a bonsai pot for all this time, and now has a lovely shape, with nice, dense branches. It was last repotted around a year ago in this Gordon Duffett container.

The design of this bonsai is slightly unconventional, and it breaks many of the rules, but it works well because it looks absolutely natural. It is one of my particular favourites, and has great sentimental value.

A 40- to 50-year-old *Larix*.

HINOKI CYPRESS

ROOT-OVER-ROCK STYLE

In theory, any species of tree can be trained in the root-over-rock, but, in practice, only a few varieties are used, either because the others are too difficult to train or because there is no market for them. Hinoki cypresses are trained in this way, however: this group of five trees having been trained over this piece of Japanese sandstone for the best part of 50 years.

The group was imported from Japan in the early 1960s. Originally it consisted of seven trees, but over the years two have died from lack of light. The remaining five are extremely healthy, though. The canopy of foliage is very dense because each year's growth is so vigorous, and the shoots have to be pinched constantly in order to keep the trees compact. The group has a beautiful outline: in fact, it resembles a single tree rather than five separate trees that have been planted together. This feeling of coherence is essential to the success of a group planting.

Hinoki cypresses should be shaded in order to keep their foliage looking fresh, and in the winter shading is also necessary to prevent frost-burn.

Five *Chamaeaecyparis obtusa.*

COTONEASTER

ROOT-OVER-ROCK STYLE

The common garden or rock cotoneaster *(Cotoneaster horizontalis)* makes an extremely nice bonsai, and is attractive all the year round. In spring it grows lovely pink and white flowers that attract bees, while the foliage starts off a lovely shade of green, and turns to brilliant scarlet in the autumn. The beautiful red berries are also very attractive and remain on the tree throughout the winter, and sometimes even last well into the Spring.

Cotoneasters are hardy little trees, and can be trained into most of the styles used in bonsai, including group plantings. They continue to flower and berry with very little care and attention. But to ensure a good crop of berries each year, you should feed the tree regularly, from June right through to early September. Any good fruiting or flowering tree fertilizer, such as rose or tomato fertilizer, is suitable. The other requirement for growing cotoneasters is that they should be repotted each year, because they are so vigorous: otherwise, their vigour will be lost, and the branches might die back.

This cotoneaster has been grown in the root-over-rock style, with the roots draped with the rock and the branches arranged to form a very pleasing triangular shape.

Cotoneaster horizontalis.

CHINESE JUNIPER

MULTIPLE-TREE-ON-ROCK STYLE

These two Chinese junipers were planted on this piece of rock 15 years ago. The result is a very pleasing composition, which works well because it looks absolutely natural; it can best be described as grown in the multiple-tree-on-rock style.

Junipers have a number of specific requirements when grown as bonsai. First, they regularly need to be pinched back hard, in order to keep the clouds of foliage tight. If this is neglected, the shoots become long and straggly, and this spoils the outline of the tree. Second, they do not like "wet feet". If their roots are water-logged the tree will soon die, so a free-draining compost is absolutely essential for good health. The growing medium used for this tree consists of 75% 5mm grit and 25% John Innes No2 compost. Third, regular feeding is vital, beginning in the early spring and continuing through until late summer.

Two *Juniperus chinensis* "Sargentii".

NANDINA

NATURAL STYLE

The *Nandina* is a very popular garden shrub in China and Japan, and is widely used in Japanese garden landscapes. In its natural habitat it can grow to become a fairly large bush. This one is the Japanese variety, which has a more lightly coloured leaf. It has been made into a bonsai from a fairly large old tree, and now has a trunk diameter of about 4.25 inches (11cm). The lovely pinnate leaves give the tree a very delicate feeling.

Nandina are sometimes treated as indoor bonsai, because they are not able to withstand very cold temperatures when planted in small pots, but they are better grown as outdoor bonsai during the summer and given some winter protection during cold spells; planted in large pots or in the ground they are quite hardy. They prefer a loamy compost and need to be fed regularly, and you should pinch the shoots at frequent intervals to stop them becoming too long and straggly.

63

Nandina domestica.

SAGERETIA

A LANDSCAPE EFFECT

The Bird Plum cherry (*Sageretia theezans*) comes from southern China, where it is often used as a hedging shrub. It is very suitable for bonsai, though, since it stands up to pruning well and it has a particularly attractive bark that resembles that of the large London Plane (*Platanus orientalis*).

Because *Sageretia* comes from southern China it is semi-tropical and so needs to be treated as an indoor bonsai. However, it can stand fairly low temperatures and I have grown the tree successful in temperatures as low as -3°C – but it must not be allowed to freeze for any prolonged period of say 48 hours or more. To be on the safe side it is better to protect the tree from frost and keep it at a minimum temperature of about 5°C.

Sageretia is an elegant tree with beautiful shiny green leaves. If grown in greenhouse conditions, at temperatures of between 10°C and 20°C, with ample humidity, the tree will produce tiny white flowers and also small berry-like fruit. As with most Chinese bonsai, this *Sageretia* has been planted in a shallow Chinese pot with pieces of rock and tiny figures to create a landscape effect. Summing up what bonsai is all about – creating a picture – the Chinese refer to this effect as *Pen-jing,* or "potted scenery".

Sageretia theezans.

NANDINA

EXPOSED-ROOT STYLE

The Sacred Bamboo (*Nandina domestica*) is a fairly common shrub in the Far East. There are many different clones and each has differing growth habits. This particular variety comes from southern China, where *Nandina* are grown extensively as indoor bonsai for export; as can be seen from the trunk and leaves, *Nandina* are closely related to the *Berberis* family.

This bonsai is a particularly good example of the type. *Nandina* roots have great character, which can be shown off to good advantage in the exposed-root style.

Nandina domestica.

ZELKOVA NIRE

POLLARDED OAK

This Japanese grey bark elm (*Zelkova Nire*) tree looks much larger than it really is, because it has been trained to resemble a huge pollarded oak. In fact, the tree is only 5.9 inches (15cm) high, including its pot. It sits on a tiny, antique Chinese stand, made of rosewood with a maple wood inlay.

Small trees can have a lot of character if they are trained well. Obviously, the longer they are trained the more refined they become, and so the more convincing as bonsai. But the skill of the bonsai artist is also important. This tree has only been trained for a year, but already has a good structure. It can be kept at this size for the next 10 to 15 years by constant clipping and repotting once every other year. In time, the head of the tree will become more dense and twigginess will become the most attractive feature.

Deciduous trees such as this are best viewed in the winter without foliage: it is then that the fine ramification of the branches can be fully appreciated.

Zelkova nire.

BAMBOO

BUDDHA'S BELLY

Bamboo is said to have a million uses: its young shoots are a gourmet's delight; it provides shade from the sun; the mature stems can be used for making boats, baskets, scaffold poles and so on. And bamboo makes a delightful subject for bonsai, too. The dwarf varieties of bamboo, which resemble fine grasses, are extensively used for "accent plantings", and tall, woody-stemmed varieties are cut down for use as traditional bonsai; the variety of bamboo known as "Buddha's Belly", which consists of a series of waisted stems, is often grown in China because it looks so unusual.

Apart from its more practical uses, bamboo has many evocative qualities. The sound of bamboo leaves rustling in the gentle breeze symbolizes the idyllic life, and, similarly, a bonsai created from bamboo evokes a sense of peace and calm. This bamboo bonsai is displayed in a room setting: it has a cool and elegant appearance that never fails to give enjoyment to all who see it.

Arundinaria "Buddha's Belly".

NANDINA

CLUMP STYLE

The stumps of *Nandina* are full of character and are used extensively for making clump-style indoor bonsai. This clump has been planted in an ultra-modern pot and is displayed against a Japanese folding screen. It has a cool, elegant look, and a distinctly oriental flavour – in fact, the arrangement resembles a modern Japanese flower arrangement.

New shapes and styles are not often seen in bonsai, because the art tends to be entrenched in old traditions. But it is important to experiment with new ideas, as some bonsai artists are beginning to do, and it is only by doing this that the art can grow.

A *Nandina* in a modern pot.

TRIDENT MAPLE

THICK-TRUNK STYLE

O ver the last few years thick-trunked trees seem to have become fashionable. This was not always the case, as one can see from the bonsai albums produced in the late 50s and early 60s. In those days, elegance and antiquity were not always associated with trunk girth. But trees with thick trunks are now very popular, probably because they convey an image of power and dynamism.

Trident maples are extremely vigorous growers, so relatively young trees can develop a thick trunk in just a few years. This tree, imported by Heron's Nursery in 1987, is no more than 30 years old and was probably grown from a seed or cutting. The flair of its roots is exquisite, and the massive buttress root and lovely taper are impressive, to say the least. This photograph was taken in the early spring, and the tree is just breaking dormancy – the image is of a mighty giant waking from his sleep.

Acer buerginarium.

TRIDENT MAPLE

FORMAL-UPRIGHT STYLE

This specimen trident maple (*Acer buergerianum*) has been grown in the formal upright style. It is about 24.5 inches (62cm) high and has been trained in a bonsai pot for most of its 40 years or so life. A look at the fairly mature branches shows that the tree has been considerably refined, and also reveals that a beautiful buttress root is starting to develop.

As with most deciduous bonsai, this maple is best appreciated during the winter, when it has no leaves, and its beautiful trunk taper and general elegance can be clearly seen. Despite the fact that trident maples are normally masculine-looking, with thick trunks, this true has a surprisingly feminine character.

Acer buergerianum.

MOUNTAIN MAPLE

A SURREY OAK IMAGE

In bonsai, the effect of a tree does not necessarily have to reflect the character of that tree when full-grown in its natural habitat. Junipers, for example, are often used to creating pine images, while maples can be used for creating images of other deciduous species.

This massive mountain maple is one of the largest bonsai in my collection – its trunk is 5.9 inches (15cm) in diameter, and it is 3.25 feet (1m) in height and width. Now well over 100 years old, it has been grown to resemble the massive oak trees that grow in the Surrey countryside where we live – the heavy trunk, which has rotted through over the years, is just like the ancient, 500-year-old oak in our local village.

The tree was restyled 4 years ago, when two superfluous branches were removed from halfway up the trunk – the procedure has left a scar that should heal over in time – and the back of the composition was turned into the front, because the root structure is more interesting on this side.

Judged by classical bonsai standards, the tree has a number of faults, but its immense presence overrides these considerations – certainly for visitors to our nursery, who find it one of their favourite trees.

Acer palmatum.

JAPANESE HORNBEAM

SEMI-CASCADE STYLE

This fairly large Japanese hornbeam (*Carpinus japonica*) has been grown in a variant of the full-cascade style, in which the tip of the cascading branch does not extend beyond the edge of the pot; it is known as the semi-cascade style. The tree is about 80 years old, and was imported from Japan in the early 1960s. Now its stands about 19.5 inches (50cm) high and 3.25 feet (1m) wide in a deep, square Tokoname container.

This tree flowers and sets seed regularly: the Japanese hornbeam is a fairly vigorous tree, but unfortunately it does have the habit of losing branches suddenly. Some of the branches of this one died back a few years ago, and it had to be restyled to get it into show condition once more.

Japanese hornbeams propagate very easily from cuttings. I find softwood cuttings taken in early summer best, and these can be grown into fairly sturdy trees in a couple of years. All of the hornbeams are excellent subjects for bonsai, with one of the most vigorous being the European common hornbeam (*Carpinus betulus*).

Carpinus japonica.

JUNIPER

CASCADE STYLE

This cascade juniper, of the variety *Juniperus communis hornibrookii,* was created from ordinary garden centre material, beginning about 10 years ago. The main trunk is now around 23.5 inches (60cm) long.

The composition is rather unconventional, in that there are three cascading trunks. It works well, though, because the branches are rather sparse and this helps to fill out the tree. The trunk line is sinuous and graceful, too, which helps lend character to what would otherwise be a fairly ordinary bonsai.

Juniperus communis hornibrookii.

SCOTS PINE

CASCADE STYLE

The cascade style of bonsai simulates trees that in nature grow out of sheer rock faces. Such trees can usually be seen wherever outcrops of rock occur. In hilly and mountainous regions these trees are more dramatic in appearance, because they have been lashed by the elements and consequently have gnarled and twisted shapes. In order to be convincing, a good cascade bonsai should be able to recreate these effects on a miniature scale.

I made this cascade tree from a young Scots Pine (*Pinus sylvestris*) that I collected 15 years ago, when it was probably already about 10 years old, and now it is planted in a beautiful, buff-glazed stoneware pot made by Gordon Duffett.

Cascade trees are generally quite difficult to keep in good condition, because the growing tip of the tree tends to become weak. The crown, or apex, is usually more vigorous and has to be constantly pinched in order to prevent it depriving the lower branches of nourishment. It is worth persevering, though, because the cascade is a very elegant style and has long been popular with Chinese and Japanese bonsai artists alike. By tradition, most cascade trees are made from coniferous species, but there is no reason why the deciduous varieties may not be used for this style. Even flowering trees can make extremely beautiful cascade subjects.

Pinus sylvestris.

FIRETHORN

ROOT-OVER-ROCK STYLE

This common Firethorn (*Pyracantha angustifolia*) is about 25 years old and stands 25.5 inches (65cm) high; it has been trained in the root-over-rock style. The main attraction of this bonsai is probably its lovely red berries, although it also has a number of other interesting facets. In spring the tree is smothered with creamy-white flowers, and this display is followed in the autumn by a heavy crop of berries. The berries last well into the next spring, if kept away from the birds.

The Firethorn is a beautiful tree, but it does need regular attention: it is an extremely vigorous shrub, so requires constant pruning in order to keep it in good shape.

Pyracantha angustifolia.

MAPLE

MULTIPLE-TRUNK STYLE

As with all other bonsai styles the multi-trunk style derives its inspiration from nature. This five-trunk maple is reminiscent of the multi-trunk trees that grow in natural woodlands – silver birch and hazel tend to grow in this way.

Multiple-trunk bonsai can be created in a number of ways. They may be grown by "stooling" – that is, cutting a deciduous tree down to ground level and letting it spring up again – or by putting together a number of separate trees that will in time fuse together at the base to look like a single tree. This maple clump has been made by the latter method. The composition is very natural, with the positioning of the trees on the left and the empty space on the right giving it a good balance, and the shallow container sets off the slender trunks well.

A five-trunk *Acer palmatum.*

TRIDENT MAPLE

TWIN-TRUNK STYLE

Several varieties of trident maple have been developed over the years, some with cork bark and others with variegated leaves. This one has beautiful cream-coloured leaves that are streaked with green and pink. Unfortunately, though, it tends to be scorched by strong sunlight and frost.

The tree has a very elegant shape and is grown in the twin-trunk style; it stands 28.25 inches (72cm) high. Although the tree has beautiful structure, its main attraction is probably its lovely foliage.

A variegated *Acer buergerianum.*

CHAMAECYPARIS

FOREST STYLE

T his forest of seven tall trees – the variety being *Chamaecyparis pisifera* "Boulevard" – was created four years ago from ordinary garden centre material. It is a huge arrangement, with the tallest tree standing 41.25 inches (105cm) high. Despite its size, however, the tree looks very light and airy, with the composition looking very natural.

Most varieties of *Chamaecyparis pisifera* can be used for making bonsai. They should be pinched back regularly in order to keep the foliage pads tight, and the unsightly dead foliage that tends to accumulate inside the branches should be removed regularly if the tree is to look green and healthy. Apart from these minor problems, the Boulevard is a fairly robust species. It is not at all demanding and can withstand both very high and very low temperatures. In the winter, frost can discolour the foliage slightly, turning it reddish brown, but it soon greens up again in the spring.

A large arrangement such as this should be turned round at regular intervals, so that it gets light from all sides. This prevents the branches at the back of the group from dying back.

Chamaecyparis pisifera "boulevard".

SHIKOKU WHITE PINE

INFORMAL-UPRIGHT STYLE

This Japanese White pine comes from Shikoku Island, in south-west Japan. The gnarled, old look is created by leaving the training wires embedded in the trunk so that the bark surface swells. Like most white pines, this one has been grafted on to black pine root stock, which makes for a much more vigorous tree. Japanese white pines that are grown on their own roots are not as vigorous, and their colour is not as good. This specimen has a vibrant blue-grey colour that becomes even more pronounced in the early spring.

Pines and junipers are very long-lived trees: there are many examples of white pine in Japan that are several hundred years old. This tree is really quite juvenile when compared to some of these magnificent specimens, since it is only 20 years old and 17.5 inches (45cm) high. Its style comes closest to being informal upright, and its drum pot has been chosen to match its rugged appearance.

Pinus pinta phylla.

TRIDENT MAPLE

MULTI-TRUNK STYLE

This trident maple, grown in the root-over-rock style, was imported from Japan in the early 1960s and is about 100 years old. The tree is large, being 24.5 inches (62cm) wide and 21.5 inches (55cm) high, and extremely heavy – it takes two strong men to move it. The tree is unique for a number of reasons: first, not many root-over-rock trident maples are grown in this style, which can best be described as partly multi-trunk and partly broom; and, second, a sandstone rock has been used rather than Ibigawa volcanic rock, which is the traditional rock for developing trident maples in this fashion.

This tree is affectionately called "the Hedgehog" by British bonsai enthusiasts because of its rounded shape, and has been exhibited at the Chelsea Flower Show on a number of occasions.

The "Hedgehog" looks very powerful, with roots and trunk like the rippling muscles of a bodybuilder, yet with fine branches that convey a sense of finesse that only comes with constant clipping over many, many years. The tree is still extremely vigorous despite its age and is repotted once every other year. It is possible that, in fact, this tree comprises several trees that have been planted together to give the impression of a single, twisted trunk.

Acer buergerianum.

KIYOHIME MAPLE

BROOM STYLE

This is one of the *Yatsabusa,* or dwarf Japanese maples (*Acer palmatum "Kiyohime"*). They are slow-growing shrubs by nature, and when trained as bonsai they grow even more slowly; they have been known to grow no more than half an inch (1.27cm) a year in a bonsai pot.

The Kiyohime maple is perhaps the only variety of maple that is suitable for training in the broom style. This is because it has a very dense twig structure, that makes it very suitable for viewing in the winter when it is bare of all its leaves. This particular tree is between 25 and 30 years old and has a spread of 9.8 inches (25cm). It has been planted in a modern stoneware ceramic container in order to emphasize its rounded shape.

Acer palmatum "Kiyohime".

ZELKOVA SERRATA

BROOM STYLE

Japanese grey bark elm (Zelkova serrata) is the traditional variety of tree used for the broom style of bonsai. As with most deciduous trees, broom style *zelkova* are grown mainly with an eye to the way they look during winter. It is only when the tree has shed all its leaves that the fine tracery of branches can be fully admired.

This particular tree is 13.4 inches (34cm) high and the container is 19.7 inches (50cm) in diameter. The container is not a conventional one – in fact, it is a modern sculpture crafted in stoneware pottery. Rather more conventionally, though, the tree has taken nearly 27 years to develop from seed. Good *Zelkova* brooms cannot be hurried in any way, and there are no short cuts to making fine broom-style trees. It is only through meticulous pinching and pruning that the fine ramification of branches develops. Feeding and repotting are very carefully controlled, so as not to encourage coarse or over-vigorous growth: this would spoil the very delicate character of the tree. As a result, broom-style bonsai are truly connoisseur's trees.

Zelkova serrata.

NISHIKI BLACK PINE

BARK SHAPES

The "Nishiki", or cork bark black pine, is grown primarily for its very interesting bark. This is deeply ridged, and as the tree gets older the ridges become more pronounced and develop in large irregularly shaped wings. Indeed bonsai of this variety are judged for the quality of their bark: the deeper and more interesting the bark shapes, the more highly prized the tree. This example is about 30 years old, and measures 27.5 inches (70cm) high. It is by no means a classic bonsai, as the wings have not yet developed fully – some of the Nishiki black pines in Japan have wings that are 6 to 8 inches (15-20cm) thick. But, given another 20 years or so, it could begin to look like a classic.

Nishiki black pine are grown in large numbers on Shikoku Island in Japan, where most of the Japanese black and white pines originate. There you can see field upon field of pine bonsai in various stages of development. Both the Japanese black pine (*Pinus thunbergii*) and Japanese white pine (*Pinus pentaphylla*) are slightly fragile, in that they cannot stand prolonged spells of hard frost. They are need the shelter of a cool greenhouse in the cooler temperate climate of northern Europe and North America, with a very sandy, well-drained compost and not too much water.

Pinus thunbergii.

MAME JUNIPER

CASCADE STYLE

Not all bonsai have to be large to be impressive. Small bonsai, too, can be very beautiful. This little Chinese juniper "mame", or "small bonsai", is only 2.75 inches (7cm) high, and was grown from a cutting taken from one of my bigger Chinese juniper bonsai during the course of pruning. It could stay this size for around next 10 years or so if it is repotted regularly to keep it in good health, but it will, of course, require constant feeding to maintain its vigour and colour. In time the trunk will thicken; when it does become more mature it will resemble some of the old junipers that grow out of the cliffs and rock precipices in the mountains of Japan and the Alps.

Deep "cascade pots" are used for this style of tree – a shallow container would not be appropriate as the tree would not be able to hang over the side in cascade fashion. Remember that the choice of pot is all part of the aesthetics of bonsai design.

Juniperus chinensis "Sargentii".

SAWARA CYPRESS

MAME BONSAI

Sawara cypresses (*Chamaecyparis pisifera*) are very suitable subjects for bonsai treatment, being particularly good for small, or "Mame", bonsai. That being so, it seems a pity that they are not more widely used as a variety for bonsai, as they are extremely hardy and their trunks have a very interesting texture. They are sometimes developed as large specimen trees, although not often exhibited.

This little tree is only about 3 inches (8cm) high. It is planted in a modern ceramic stoneware container, a setting that makes this small tree look like a much larger tree growing on the brow of a hill.

Contemporary sculptural containers such as this are not often used by bonsai enthusiasts, as they are considered too distracting. But if the tree and container form a harmonious entity, there is no reason why it should not be successful. I believe that just as in Ikebana, where contemporary containers and materials are now being used on a much wider scale, so in bonsai one needs to develop new concepts and approaches to design in order to enable the art to grow.

Chamaecyparis pisifera.

ZELKOVA MAKINO

INFORMAL-UPRIGHT STYLE

A *Zelkova makino* grown in the informal-upright style. This massive bonsai is 27.5 inches (70cm) high, and its pot alone measures 19.6 inches by 13.7 inches (50cm x 35cm): a very powerful looking tree indeed, yet the huge trunk and heavy buttress roots contrast sharply with the very fine branches and twigs. Surprisingly, the tree is probably between 50 and 60 years old, which is is relatively young by traditional bonsai standards.

This variety of *Zelkova* closely resembles the Chinese Elm (*Ulmus parviflora*), but with leaves that are variegated and have saw-tooth edges. It is a delightful tree when it is just coming into leaf, but it needs protection from frosts and strong winds in order to avoid windburn, and from strong sunshine that can scorch the leaves, so it is best grown under shading.

Zelkova makino.

THREE ZELKOVAS

GROUP STYLE

This group of three small Japanese grey bark elms (*Zelkova serrata*) is 11.8 inches (30cm) high. The pot is a contemporary one sculpted in stoneware clay. The composition finds its inspiration from the type of winter landscape often seen in southern England: the *Zelkovas* in this picture could easily be English elms, silhouetted against the clear, blue sky of winter, and the surface of the pot has been made to resemble the furrows on a freshly ploughed field.

Bonsai is all about creating images and pictures of the scenery that one comes across in nature, using the medium of living plant material. This particular composition was created a few months ago: I arranged the trees so as to achieve perspective, balance and depth, then set them off with a beautiful sculpted pot.

Three *Zelkova serrata.*

SCOTS PINE

LITERATI STYLE

This literati-style Scots pine (*Pinus sylvestris*) has been in training for the last six years, having been collected in the wild when it was just a stray seedling, around three years old, by the roadside. It might well have been trampled over, or cleared by foresters, but after much patience and loving care it is has now been transformed into something quite beautiful, around 15.7 inches (40cm) high.

Literati-style trees, called *bunjin* by the Japanese, are admired for the artistic lines of their trunks. The flow and rhythm of these trunks is reminiscent of the brush strokes of Chinese ink wash paintings. Pictures of pine trees grown in this style used to preoccupy Chinese scholars for centuries: in fact, the term "literati" is named after the Chinese scholars who went to live in mountain retreats simply to admire nature and to engage in artistic pursuits. These Chinese scholars played a very significant part in influencing the development of bonsai aesthetics as we know it today.

Pinus sylvestris.

JAPANESE HORNBEAM

INFORMAL-UPRIGHT STYLE

A Japanese hornbeam (*Carpinus laxiflora*), grown in the informal-upright style. This specimen tree was imported from Japan in 1987, and is now about 50 years old and 25.6 inches (65cm) high.

This bonsai has a very natural shape and resembles a fully grown hornbeam in the wild. The tree's bark has a lovely colour and very interesting texture, while vertical striations give the trunk an added interest. The taper is excellent, too, being broad at the base and decreasing gradually towards the top. In bonsai parlance, this tree has elegance and movement.

Carpinus laxiflora.

JUNIPER RIGIDA

INFORMAL-UPRIGHT STYLE

Junipers are a favourite subject for bonsai. This particular variety, *Juniperus rigida "yatsabusa"*, has very short needles that are bluish-grey in colour and, unlike those of the more common variety of *rigida,* are not sharp.

The *yatsabusa* variety is a fairly rapid grower: this example is 29 inches (74cm) high and is no more than 20 years old. It has been trained in the informal-upright style, with the foliage pads arranged in neat clumps. Constant pinching of the foliage tips is needed to keep the tree smart and well groomed.

Juniperus rigida "yatsabusa".

NEEDLE JUNIPER

A 300-YEAR-OLD TREE

I f ever there was a grand old tree of British Bonsai, this must be the one. It has appeared on television on a number of occasions and it attracts the most interest whenever it is displayed at the Chelsea Flower Show. This needle juniper (*Juniperus rigida*) is estimated to be at least 300 years old. It was imported from Japan nearly 30 years ago and has been in my personal collection for the past 11 years.

I have altered the tree's shape quite considerably since I have had it. The front has been changed round and the leader grown on much more. The tree has immense presence, largely on account of its sheer size and, of course, the superb driftwood effects. There is very little live bark left on the tree, yet it is still as vigorous as ever. The tree is 3.25 feet (1m) high and 46.5 inches (118cm) wide, but, despite its size, the tree is said to have a very feminine, graceful character.

Juniperus rigida.

SAN JOSE JUNIPER

DRIFTWOOD EFFECTS

This juniper was designed by Bonsai Master John Naka when he visited Britain in 1984. It was created from a tree that I had dug up two years previously from a friend's garden. Only one of the original five branches was used to make this bonsai – the rest were discarded, and the stubs used for creating the driftwood effects, with lot of jins and shari. As with most trees that have driftwood, the impression given here is of rugged power.

This variety of juniper has a very coarse growth, and tends to lose its foliage colour when left out in the heat of the sun; it is also quite easily burnt by the frost. However, the foliage greens up well when the tree kept n the shade.

Juniperus chinensis "San Jose".

JAPANESE BLACK PINE

INFORMAL-UPRIGHT STYLE

The Japanese black pine (*Pinus thunbergii*) is a rugged looking tree with rough bark and coarse needles. It is also a vigorous grower, thriving in warm conditions but also having the ability to withstand fairly cold winters. This 100-year-old tree is kept out in the open all the year round and has withstood temperatures as low as - 15°C with no ill effects.

Imported from Japan in the early 1960s, the tree is now 30.7 inches (80cm) high and has been trained in the informal-upright style. It is repotted once every five or six years, on the last occasion being two years ago, when it was put into this lovely Gordon Duffett container. This is one of the favourite trees in my collection and one that will probably never be sold.

Pinus thunbergii.

TRIDENT MAPLE

TWIN-TRUNK STYLE

A large trident maple, grown in the twin-trunk style, which stands 27.5 inches (70cm) high and 21.6 inches (55cm) wide, with a trunk diameter of 7.5 inches (19cm).

As with most trident maples, this tree has a very powerful and chunky look. Now between 45 and 50 years old, it was probably grown rapidly in the initial stage of its development but the branches and trunk taper have been developed slowly over the last 10 to 15 years. Notice the fine overall triangular shape of the canopy, which envelopes both the main and the subsidiary trunk. The apex of the two trunks are in complete harmony with each other and they both flow in the same direction – towards the right. The branches have good refinement and are well tiered.

When developed as bonsai, trident maples are used to create images of gnarled old trees with very heavy trunks, such as the mighty English oaks and the oriental plane tree. Being a maple, this tree has beautiful autumn foliage, with soft pink and orange hues. The tree is lovely to look at both when in full leaf and when without its leaves.

Acer buergerianum.

JAPANESE WHITE PINE

INFORMAL-UPRIGHT STYLE

These delightful Japanese white pines (*Pinus pentaphylla*) are about 12 years old, and are 9.5 inches (24cm) tall with a trunk diameter of about an inch (2.5cm). They are all grafted onto root stock from black pines and were field-grown for the first four or five years of training. In the bonsai growing regions of Japan, field upon field of these dwarf pines can be seen growing in serried ranks.

Small bonsai such as these have enormous potential. They may be grown on to become larger specimens, or refined into small specimen bonsai with lots of interesting detail. White pines grown in this informal-upright style are extremely popular, perhaps because they are what most people imagine a bonsai to be. They are fairly hardy subjects but need to be protected from hard frosts; ideally, they should not be exposed to frosts at all, since the climate in southern Japan, where these pines originated, is almost Mediterranean.

Pinus pentaphylla.

BONSAI TECHNIQUES

Growing Up and Growing Down Methods –
Shaping Bonsai – Cutting and Trimming – Wiring –
Pots – Soils – Feeding and – General Care –
Driftwood Effects – Display and Exhibition.

INDEX and ACKNOWLEDGEMENTS

This 7-year-old bonsai is of the variety – *Juniper media* "Blauws". Having been – repotted each year, it is now 33.5 inches (85cm) high and 29.5 inches – (75cm) wide, and has considerable charisma despite the fact that it has not been trained for long.

GROWING UP AND GROWING DOWN

In recent years many books have been written on various aspects of bonsai. Some have dealt with general principles whilst others have touched on the more detailed and advanced techniques. Each has contributed in its own special way to the increasing fund of knowledge on this subject.

In a book such as this, where the main objective is to provide inspiration for the keen bonsai grower, it is impossible to cover in depth all the various techniques of growing and refining bonsai.

So this section is intended to serve as a quick reference guide to the various tools and techniques that are now available to the bonsai enthusiast, and to help to widen the horizons of those who are new to the pastime. But I hope that it will encourage all bonsai enthusiasts to become more adventurous in their attempts to create beautiful trees.

Techniques are, of course, only the means by which the desired end-result is achieved. The inspiration for a good bonsai must emanate first and foremost from the soul of the artist. But techniques are nevertheless extremely important, since they are the mechanism by which ideas are transformed into reality. The more skilled and accomplished the artist is in the use of the various techniques, the more successful will be the bonsai created. And they will also bear the stamp of his or her own personal style.

THE BASICS
There are basically two approaches to making bonsai: first, to grow the bonsai up – that is, to develop young seedlings to the appropriate size; second, to cut down a larger and more mature tree to "grow a bonsai down" from the stump that is left.

Each method has its advantages and drawbacks. The first is a slow

From the left: a 6-week-old crab apple; a 6-year-old zelkova; and a 2-year-old larch. All were "grown up" from seedlings.

process but the results are more refined; the second is a quicker method but lacks the refinement that time alone can produce. Whichever method is adopted – one must recognize that patience and skill is needed as there are no real shortcuts to achieving excellence.

STARTER MATERIAL: SEEDLINGS

The three examples of juvenile starter material illustrated on the left-hand page are all ideal subjects for the "growing up" method of training bonsai.

The little zelkova, in the middle of the photograph, is a six-year-old seedling that has been grown in a pot all its life. Using a pot helps the tree to develop fine twigs; if the zelkova had been planted in the ground, it would have become much thicker in the trunk but the branches would have very little refinement.

This example could be trained in the broom style by progressively potting it on into a slightly larger container. However, the branch tips would need to be constantly pinched in order to encourage side shoots to develop, and, in time, this

This classic cotoneaster, created by Japanese Bonsai Master John Naka in 1984, started life two years previously as a stump dug up from a Surrey garden.

GROWING UP AND GROWING DOWN/2

would create a very dense head of twigs.

The larch seedling, on the right, is only two years old. It should be encouraged to grow on by potting it into a larger container, so that the trunk and branches will thicken. These can then be wired and shaped over the next few years. Some very nice larch bonsai can be produced from seed in as little as 7 or 8 years.

The crab-apple seedlings are only six-weeks old. From this time, each seedling will be pricked out and grown on in an individual pot. By judicious pinching and pruning of the growing shoots, chunky little trees will develop, and they will be ready to be induced to flower in about five or six years' time.

Of course, there is no reason why any of these three subjects should not be allowed to grow vigorously, simply by planting them in the ground and leaving them for a few years for their trunks to thicken. When they are thick

Peter Chan with an elm stump dug from his nursery fields. It was cut down three years ago, immediately after planting, allowed to grow, then cut down again each year before being potted: the "growing down" method of producing bonsai.

enough to be made into bonsai, they can be chopped down to the appropriate height and developed into bonsai by the "growing down" method.

STARTER MATERIALS: STUMPS

The photograph on these pages shows an English elm stump that we have dug up recently from our nursery fields. The stump is 4 inches (10cm) in diameter at the base; the discarded tree was 2.2 yards (2m) high and 2 inches (5cm) diameter when it was planted in the ground three years ago.

Immediately after planting it was cut down to 2 feet (0.6m) and a new leader encouraged to grow. The following year the leader was cut down again a few inches above the previous years cut and another leader allowed to develop. By progressively cutting each year's new leader, a gradual tapering of the trunk was achieved. The stump was dug up when it had thickened sufficiently, and it will be placed in a pot to develop the final shape of the bonsai.

This method of developing bonsai is now widely practised all over the world, because it is relatively quick. Trees with thick, chunky trunks can be produced in a matter of a few years and they are very convincing as mature bonsai.

Small alpine plants – here a variety of *Sempervivum* – are not really bonsai *per se*, when planted in bonsai pots, but do play a part in the tradition of the art. Known as "accent plantings", they are placed with large bonsai trees both to represent the seasons and to emphasize scale.

SHAPING BONSAI

The shapes of most bonsai are achieved artificially. Even in the case of a collected specimen, where most of the work has already been done by nature, some final shaping is still necessary to give a tree character.

Shaping can be performed in two ways: by cutting or by bending. At one time, most shaping of bonsai was done by the clip and grow method – but this was a slow and tedious business. Modern techniques are much faster, making extensive use of wire. Either copper or aluminium wire can be used; both are equally acceptable, although there is a trend now to use copper, as it has been found to hold the shape of branches and trunks rather better than its aluminium counterpart.

A wide variety of specialist bonsai tools is available for the enthusiast. Many of them are extremely useful; nevertheless, extremely sophisticated bonsai can be created with nothing more than a scissors, wire and wire-cutters.

SCISSORS

Bonsai scissors come in all shapes and sizes. As with most tools, the good quality ones are very expensive. They are extremely sharp but they must be properly cared for if they are to give long and useful service. Sharpen them with an oil stone from time to time, in order to keep the cutting edge keen.

There is a trend now towards stainless steel bonsai tools, however. These are expensive, but worth buying, because they stay sharp for much longer and never rust. Some scissors are even spring-loaded – very useful when a lot of snipping and pruning has to be done.

The long-handled scissors shown here are used for trimming twigs. They enable you to reach right inside the branch structure without getting entangled in it. The large handled, long-bladed scissors are good for general cutting work as well as for root pruning.

Two Chinese elms, grown in the popular exposed root style. Between five and six years old, these trees were raised from root cuttings, and the roots deliberately raised above the soil to create this unusual effect. Constant trimming and pruning was needed to achieve this shape, and to maintain it.

Scissors are essential tools for the bonsai artist, and it is sensible to buy the best that you can afford. A wide range of types is available, but long-handled scissors are specially useful, because they can reach right inside the branches.

CUTTING AND TRIMMING

Cutting and trimming is absolutely basic to bonsai. Unless one is prepared to cut branches and bits of trunk, it is difficult to imagine how a bonsai could be created at all.

Almost invariably, the raw material for a bonsai has a number of extraneous branches. These have to be removed in order to form the desired shapes and styles that are used in bonsai. There are a huge number of cutting tools on the market today, all of them designed to do just this.

Japanese bonsai catalogues list a wide range of tools of various shapes and sizes, each with a specific application and use. One could spend a fortune on bonsai tools alone. But creativity and skill does not depend on the

A selection of power tools and hand tools for cutting, trimming and carving. Hand tools give just as good results as power tools – if not better than them, since they are easier to control; hand tools do take longer, though. Remember that protective gear is essential when using power tools.

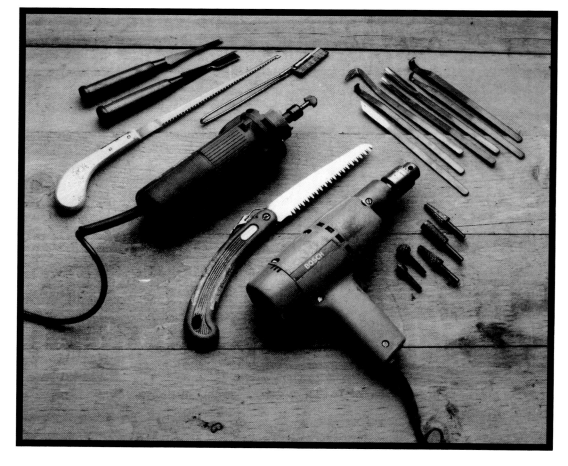

sophistication of one's implements. Very beautiful work can be done with relatively basic tools.

Carving, for example, is an important skill used in creating bonsai. Before the introduction of power tools the hand chisel reigned supreme for this. Unfortunately, though, the use of hand tools is becoming less popular, but there is no reason why this should be so. The results achieved with hand tools are easily as good.

CARE OF TOOLS

Bonsai tools should always be kept sharp. Tools that are blunt not only make the task of cutting that much more difficult, but can harm the tree as well. Always have a cleaner and oil stone handy to sharpen the cutting edge of all hand tools. And never leave steel tools in the rain, otherwise they will soon begin to rust. Even stainless steel can deteriorate if left in the open for long periods of time.

This little juniper in the cascade style was collected in the wild around five years ago, and has needed little or no training. It was found growing in a gravel scree on the side of a mountain. Such finds are rare, but by no means impossible if one is prepared to make the effort.

CUTTING AND TRIMMING/2

A selection of branch cutters and splitters. On the right is a branch splitter, made from high-quality steel; to its left, from the top down, is a "wen" cutter, a side branch cutter, a "jin" pliers and a small branch splitter. All have their special place in the art of bonsai.

Many different types of cutting implement are available, ranging from hand pruners to petrol-driven chain saws. And each and every one of these devices has its own purpose and place in bonsai.

Perhaps the most essential hand tool in bonsai is the ordinary secateurs. Next in importance comes a branch cutter, shown in action on these pages. Either flat or concave branch cutters can be used, depending on the type of cut that is desired.

BRANCH CUTTERS AND SPLITTERS

The photograph on these pages shows a selection of high quality Japanese bonsai tools for cutting branches.

The large tool on right is a branch splitter, is about 20 inches

(50cm) long and made from high-quality steel of the kind used in the manufacture of chisels and knife blades. It is used to split thick branches so that they can be bent more easily, and can also be put into service as to prune branches or roots, when necessary.

The stainless steel tool in the top left hand corner is a "wen" or knob cutter. This is used for making a concave cut after a branch has been removed – this allows a wound to callous over neatly, so that no bumps or ridges are left.

The tool below that is a side branch cutter. This allows a cut to be made very close to the trunk. The cutting edges are razor sharp and great care should be taken to ensure that they do not become blunt.

The tool second from bottom is a "jin" pliers. This has a number of uses: it can be used as pliers for finishing off wiring, but its main application is for crushing and stripping bark and wood in order to create driftwood effects. The jinning pliers is perhaps the most useful tool for making fine jins.

The tool at the bottom of the picture is a smaller type of branch splitter. In addition to its use as a branch splitter and root cutter, it can also be used for stripping dead wood in refining jins. Such tools are perhaps the most widely used of the specialist bonsai tools, because they cannot easily be

A cherry blossom bonsai. Japan's favourite flower, cherry blossom is particularly suitable for bonsai treatment, and flower prolifically. They do not need much attention, and are not fussy about fertilizers or soil.

CUTTING AND TRIMMING/3

substituted by other general gardening tools. No bonsai enthusiast should be without them.

SAWS
Saws are needed, too. They come in all shapes and sizes: the choice of which to use depends on the

thickness of the branch to be cut. There are many types of saws on the market, and the majority are ideal for bonsai work – but, again, they must be sharp to be effective. Blunt implements not only make for hard work: they can also damage a bonsai, as a result of the

A small branch splitter in use: the bonsai artist is using it to remove an extraneous branch from a small bonsai.

excessive force that has to be applied to the tree, which could damage the roots.

POWER TOOLS

Finally, there are power tools, such as routers, power chisels and chain saws. These are very useful labour-saving devices, but they are also extremely dangerous, so protective gear should always be worn– a face-shield and safety gloves are essential when using electric or petrol-driven power cutters.

It is also important to make sure that the bits used for power tools are sharp and in good condition. Nothing is more dangerous than a blunt cutting bit.

Remember, too, that power tools are not always needed. For example, hand chisels are extremely useful for sculpting and refining driftwood effects on bonsai. If they are kept clean and sharp they will give years of service.

After a branch has been removed, the "wen" cutter is used to make a concave cut on the site. This allows the wound to heal over without leaving any unsightly bumps or ridges.

WIRING

The secret of good wiring is to make it look as neat as possible. Nothing could be uglier than a mass of wires, wound in haphazard fashion around a trunk or branch.

Wire should be wound on fairly tightly and spread evenly along the length of the trunk. Always use one piece of wire to link two adjacent branches or twigs. If more than one piece of wire is needed to bend a trunk or branch, make sure that both are wound in the same direction.

Do not use more than two strands of wire: if a double strand is not strong enough to hold a branch in position, then the gauge of wire being used is too thin. In such cases, switch to a thicker gauge. If the branch still does not bend, try splitting it with a branch splitter. This might help to make the task easier.

One tip that makes wiring considerably easier is to place the bonsai on a turntable – one is shown in the photograph on this page. In fact, a turntable is one of the most useful items a bonsai artist can have. This does not need to be custom-made, but can be improvized from almost anything. The one in the photograph, for example, is made from an old office chair office chair, and is deliberately large so that it can handle the majority of the large specimen trees in my collection.

WIRE AND WIRE-CUTTERS
The wire shown in the photograph on these pages is made of anodized aluminium. This is available in a wide range of guages, from 1mm to 6 or 7mm.

Copper wire, though, is preferable: it has long been used in bonsai and is still considered by many bonsai artists to be the best type. It is easily obtainable, too: strip the copper wire from the inside of electric cables, but anneal it slightly by heating it for a short while (for 5-10 minutes, say, in a fire) before use. Be careful not to overheat copper wire, since it can become brittle.

Wire and tools, laid out ready for use on a turntable – one of the most useful items in a bonsai artist's studio. The wire shown here is made of anodized aluminium, but copper is also used – in fact, most bonsai experts prefer it. Copper wire can easily be obtained by stripping old electric cable.

Proper bonsai wire-cutters are a delight to use. The type designed for electrical use wire-cutters which electricians use are not really suitable for the purpose, because they do not have a sufficiently good cutting action. So buy purpose-made bonsai wire-cutters if your budget allows.

WIRING/2

Peter Chan wiring a larch. Wiring is one of the most time-consuming, but ultimately the most satisfying of the bonsai techniques.

Wiring is perhaps the most time-consuming of all the activities that growing bonsai involves. But it is also the most satisfying. Sometimes it can take a whole day to wire a tree, but when it is finished and the branches have been carefully arranged in position the whole tree suddenly comes alive. It is only then that the real value of meticulous wiring can be fully appreciated.

Wire should be wound on fairly tightly if it is to be effective. But it is also important to ensure that the wires are not left on for too long, or else they leave unsightly marks on the surface of the branch or trunk.

Sometimes however, wire marks can be very effective in making the bark surface look old and gnarled. This is difficult to achieve, though.

There are many misconceptions about the use of wire on trees – as can be seen at bonsai shows. Some Westerners have been led to believe that a tree should never have wires on when it goes on display, but having seen some of specimen trees on display in Japan, I am convinced that the theory has no validity.

I have seen some of the most beautiful masterpieces in Japan displayed with their wires on. The wire is hardly visible, I admit, but it certainly helps to improve the presentation of the tree.

A bird's eye view of a Hinoki Cypress in training. The tree is fairly old, so the branches are quite thick – between 0.4 and 0.8 inches (1-2cm) in diameter.

In order to shape the trunk a double strand of 4mm wire has been used, while the branches have been wired with single strands of 3mm and 4mm wire.

Trees of this age need to have the wires left on for about two to three years in order to set properly. Younger trees, on the other hand, require one growing season for the wiring to set.

POTS

By definition, a bonsai is a tree in a pot. So the pot that you choose is an integral and vital part of the entire bonsai composition. Without its pot a bonsai is incomplete.

Choosing the right pot for a tree is an art in itself. It must be the right size, shape and colour if it is to bring out the full beauty of the tree. There are many rules and conventions for the choice of pot, but in the last analysis it is the experienced eye of the bonsai artist that determines what is best.

In China and Japan, though, great store is placed on antique bonsai pots. Antique Chinese pots are highly prized in Japan and the most famous trees are usually displayed in these containers.

Most bonsai pots are made of high-fired stoneware clay, although there are a few antique Chinese pots made of porcelain. Pots to be used in colder climates should be frost-proof, and stoneware and porcelain pots meet this requirement. In the tropics, however, a frost-proof pot is not so essential, though, in fact, tradition dictates that the majority of specialist bonsai pots are made of stoneware clay.

DRAINAGE

Whatever type of pot you choose, remember that it must have good drainage. Bonsai pots made in China and Japan invariably have large drainage holes, but some contemporary pots, made in the west, only have small drainage holes. These are made by potters who do not appreciate the importance of good drainage. Do not use pots as this: good drainage is so important that it is unlikely that your bonsai will flourish in them.

This small, 12-year-old cotoneaster has been trained on a piece of Japanese volcanic rock for the last six years, and was planted to represent a tree growing out of a cliff. Tough and resilient, cotoneasters can live to be very old, but need to be pruned hard each year to maintain their shape.

Ready for potting – with good soil (made of equal parts of loam, peat and sand), a trowel and a classic pot with an adequately sized drainage hole resting on the turntable.

SOILS

This splendid forest planting of Chinese Junipers was created by the Japanese Bonsai Master John Naka on his visit to Britain in 1984. It is now one of the most valuable bonsai in Peter Chan's collection.

Volumes could be written about bonsai soil. The subject is a highly controversial one, since bonsai growers in different parts of the world have their own favourite recipes for soil.

The bonsai growers of Southern China, for example, use a thick river clay as the growing medium; the juniper growers of Japan use nothing but pure grit. All this may seem very confusing to the average bonsai grower, but with a little bit of common sense you can cut through much of the mystique that surrounds the composition of bonsai of soil can be unravelled.

As a general rule, a soil that is made up of equal parts of loam, peat and sand will do for most varieties of trees. And by observing nature, one can get to know the preferences of the different species. Azaleas and Rhododendrons, for example, love a peaty soil with some sand mixed in it. Junipers and pines, on the other hand, are sand lovers, while fruiting and flowering trees prefer a soil that is very rich in loam.

Small bonsai, such as these three delightful white pines, can be the starting point for a whole range of types of specimen bonsai. At the moment they are about 12 years old, and stand 9.8 inches (25cm) tall.

Japanese growers are particularly fond of using a red loamy soil called *akadama* soil. This comes in three grades – coarse, medium and fine. It can be used for most species of trees, but it is particularly good for the deciduous varieties.

For pines and junipers, a soil that consists predominantly of grit or sand is very good. By experimenting with different mixtures one gets to know the preferences of particular varieties of trees. And remember that different types of soil should be adapted to local growing conditions, since these can vary considerably from place to place.

But the essential requirement for good soil is efficient drainage. Unless this is available, one's efforts at growing fine bonsai will be of little use.

BONSAI CARE

Feeding is absolutely essential for a bonsai. There is much debate at present as to whether organic or inorganic fertilizers are best for bonsai. In Japan, though, many growers strike a happy medium by mixing organic and inorganic fertilizers together into a fine paste, and put this on top of their bonsai pots. The fertilizer leaches into the soil and it is efficient for the rest of the growing season.

The secret is to feed regularly, but in small amounts. In the early part of the growing season a general fertilizer such as 10:10:10 should be used; in the latter part a lower nitrogen fertilizer is preferable.

It is always better to underfeed than to overfeed your trees. A healthy tree will have a good green colour and will be better able to withstand the rigours of winter. And, as we have said, watering is vital to success: it is perhaps the single most important factor in maintaining a healthy tree. Daily watering in summer is a must, and when it is very hot it may be necessary to water two or three times a day.

REPOTTING

You should only repot your trees when they become pot-bound. As a general guide, younger trees should be repotted more frequently than older trees. Some of the well-established masterpiece bonsai are only repotted once every six or seven years, depending on how vigorously they grow. And, of course, you should only repot in the early spring.

PRUNING AND TRIMMING

Heavy branches should always be pruned in the dormant season, though twigs and young shoots can be trimmed throughout the year. When branches have been cut, the wound should always be sealed with a tree sealant – the cutpaste that Japanese growers use is extremely good for encouraging a callous to form rapidly. If a wound is not covered with sealant it takes much longer to heal over.

Constant pinching of twigs and shoots during the growing season helps to encourage density and "twigginess". Only in this way can a tree develop a good head of branches. If trees are not constantly trimmed and pinched they will soon get out of control and the shape of the tree will be lost in a very short space of time.

The apricot, or *Prunus Mume,* is one of the earliest of the cherries to come into bloom. This example is a dainty little tree, about eight years old. It has been grafted on to a common cherry root stock, and will be developed over the next few years in the semi-cascade style.

DRIFTWOOD EFFECTS

Most people think that a bonsai is a tree of great age. Part of the fascination of bonsai stems from the fact that they are gnarled old trees of great beauty and antiquity. It would seem that the older the tree, the greater its mystique and charm.

The aged look of a bonsai, however, can to a certain extent be simulated in the same way that some reproduction antique furniture can be "aged". The techniques for creating driftwood help considerably in this process.

As trees get older they often shed branches, and sometimes their trunks start to rot. Now and again they might even get struck by lightning. All these natural effects result in dead branches which in time become bleached by the weather. They all add to the character of a tree as dead

A model-maker's router is ideal for creating driftwood effects, as Peter Chan shows on this larch.

branches are invariably associated with trees which are very old, but which still struggle to survive.

Such images are of course highly romantic in Eastern philosophy and are the source of inspiration for many a fine bonsai. Over the years, bonsai with driftwood effects have come to be associated with very old trees. Of course, they are also very beautiful, too.

These driftwood effects can be created artificially. The technique is to strip the bark away from a branch or trunk and then give the exposed parts a naturally weathered look by teasing and carving the wood. The bare driftwood along the trunk is normally referred to as "shari", while the dead wood at the tips of branches is referred to as "jins".

The stripping of bark is not a difficult process, but it needs to be made to look as natural as possible.

These three chaenomeles have been grown on a piece of rock to resemble trees growing on a mountain top; the roots are all tied in with wires that have been glued on to the rock face. Rock plantings such as this need careful watering on a hot summer's day, since they can soon dry out.

DRIFTWOOD EFFECTS/2

It is also important to ensure that the bark is not removed completely from the entire circumference of the trunk, or the tree will die. The bark and the cambium beneath it is the channel through which all the nutrients to the tree is supplied. If this is cut off or interfered with in any way, then the upper portion of the tree will die.

Many of the old juniper bonsai only have a tiny sliver of live bark running from the base to the top of the tree This is usually sufficient to supply all the nutrients that are needed to keep the tree alive.

After the bark has been removed, bits of wood should be torn away carefully with a branch splitter or root pruner in order to make the jin look as if it has been created naturally. Carving chisels and model-makers' routers are ideal for refining these driftwood effects.

After carving, allow the freshly exposed wood to stand for two to three months before applying a bleaching agent. Lime sulphur has traditionally been used for bleaching and preserving dead wood, although this is becoming increasingly difficult to obtain. Some bonsai nurseries can supply lime sulphur, or a near-substitute that is equally good.

From time to time the jins and sharis should be cleaned with a stiff brush and water, in order to remove algae and moss before, applying lime sulphur again. Lime sulphur should be applied once, or perhaps twice, a year. This is best done when the wood is fairly dry. If the wood is wet it can seep into the soil and damage the roots of the tree.

A detail of the driftwood effect on a magnificent 300-year-old needle juniper (*Juniper Rigida*). These driftwood effects are all natural, and a product of age: it is jins and sharis such as these that bonsai artists attempt to imitate through carving.

DISPLAY AND EXHIBITION

All bonsai should be displayed on stands off the ground. These can either take the form of raised wooden benches or pedestals.

There are several advantages to be gained by displaying bonsai in this way. By having your trees on benches they can be viewed to the best advantage. And by raising the pots off the ground, the risks of pests and diseases entering from the ground can be reduced. Finally, raised benches also ensure air circulation and drainage for the trees, which encourages healthy growth.

Trees that are to be displayed at exhibitions must be properly groomed if they are to look their best. This involves pinching and trimming overgrown shoots, wiring branches into place and generally cleaning the trees and pots and the soil surface. Wiring should be as unobtrusive as possible, annealed copper wire is best for this purpose.

The trees ear-marked for shows also benefit from a dose of quick-acting fertilizer to green up the foliage. This should be applied about a month before they are displayed.

During the height of summer, when the sun is at its strongest, trees benefit from being placed in the shade, under netting, to prevent their leaves from being scorched. Similarly, in the winter the more tender species, such as maples and junipers, should be kept in a cold greenhouse or light, airy shed to protect them from severe frosts.

LAST THOUGHTS

Bonsai is a fascinating pastime. Not only is it creative, but it is extremely relaxing as well.

Even from its earliest days, the ancient Chinese and Japanese found peace, tranquillity and beauty in bonsai. These objectives are still valid in today's busy world. Millions of people already derive immense pleasure from bonsai. It is my hope that the reader will be inspired to take up the hobby too, and that those who are already bonsai artists will be encouraged to develop their art.

Since the word "bonsai" literally means "a tree in a pot", it is not surprising that the style of pot chosen is important to the success of a composition. This selection of classic pots shows a range of types, each of which will enhance a specific style of tree.

INDEX

ACKNOWLEDGEMENTS

The inspiration for this, my fourth book on bonsai, has been derived from the specimen trees that have been in my collection for many years. Also featured are some of the specimens imported by our Nursery – Herons Bonsai – more recently. These beautiful trees are a constant source of enjoyment and inspiration to all those who visit Herons, and we are glad that the wider public can now enjoy them through the beautiful pictures taken by photographer Don Wood.

I would like to thank my wife Dawn again for her invaluable help in transcribing the text on to computer disc: without her skills, the publisher's deadline would never have been met.

My thanks also to David Higham for his help in the nursery during the photographic sessions.

Peter Chan.